Guinea Pig Education

2 Cobs Way
New Haw, Addlestone
Surrey
KT15 3AF
Tel: 01932 336553
Website: www.guineapigeducation.co.uk

© Copyright 2013

NO part of this publication may be reproduced, stored or copied for commercial purposes and profit without the prior written permission of the publishers.

ISBN: 978-1-907733-19-2

Written by: Adele Seviour
Edited by: Sally and Amanda Jones
Graphic Design and Illustrations by: Annalisa Jones

For

Rebecca, Joshua, Michelle, Kristina, Nicole, Fleur, Tyler and Harlyn

The tabby cat with his pattern of dark markings, spots or stripes on a paler background is the oldest known domestic cat, known as felis catus to the Romans. This time his magic whiskers whisk him away for a glimpse of the Roman army.

Horace lay in the sun on the garden wall. His tabby coat rippled like little grey and white waves on a pond. His whiskers began to twitch. They twitched faster. Was he ready for take off? He activated his i-collar. Horace was a magic cat. He was a time traveller.

Horace woke up with a start. He found himself curled up by a large flat rock. Bang! Clang! He thought, "What was that noise?" Peering round the rock with wide eyes, he saw some men dropping iron shields by the roadside. Horace had travelled back to Britain in 60 AD. They were Roman foot soldiers.

There were eight men in total (a contubernium) and they were just sitting down for some lunch of corn and beans. Horace picked up the scent. He pondered, "Were they friendly?" The smell of food was too tempting so he padded up to one of the soldiers who was sitting on his cloak. "Miaow!" he begged. "Try some of this," said the soldier. Horace was hungry and wolfed it down in a few gulps. Delicious!

Horace looked at what the Roman soldiers were wearing. The Roman soldier was wearing a full army kit.

His armour was made of thin strips of metal, filled with hooks and hinges.

His metal helmet had hinged cheek pieces and a metal rim sticking out at the back.

He carried a purse on his wrist. He could only open it if he took it off, so no one could rob him.

He had metal shoulder pads.

His armour had metal breastplates.

Under his body armour, there was a rough woollen tunic.

In his leather scabbard, the Roman soldier had a large sword and daggers.

His leather belt had metal strips hanging from it.

He wore strong leather strip sandals. The sole of the shoe had patterns of iron hobnails, so they could take the weight of the soldier wearing his armour and doing miles of marching.

Armour – clothing to protect the body from harm.

Scabbard – a holder for a sword or dagger.

Hinges – attach things

"**ATTENTION**!" shouted the commanding officer, "put your packs on your shoulder ready to march, left, right - left, right." The packs looked heavier than a school bag to Horace. What was in them?

There was:

- A TOOL KIT

- A BAG OF NAILS

- ENOUGH FOOD RATIONS TO LAST THREE DAYS, INCLUDING BREAD, CHEESE, BEANS, BACON AND WATER

- A CLOAK THAT WAS ALSO A BLANKET.

Each man also needed his own tools to build camps, forts and roads. He needed:

- AN AX

- A ROPE

- A COOKING PAN AND CUP

- A TURF CUTTER, A SPADE AND A PICK AXE

- 2 POINTED STAKES TO MAKE CAMP WALLS

- A JAVELIN, A DAGGER, A SHORT SWORD CALLED A GALDIUS AND HIS RECTANGULAR SHIELD

"Ouch! I could not carry all of that," said Horace to no one in particular.

Horace padded along with the legion (a band of Roman soldiers).

"Come on puss," said the kind soldier, "march with us. We have been sent to find some clear, dry land to build a safe camp for the night, that will protect us from wild animals and surprise raids."

It was hard for Horace to keep up, so he jumped up onto the soldier's shoulder pack. "Left, right - left, right! Halt!" ordered the commanding officer. It was time to dig a camp. Horace scrabbled in the soil to help the soldiers build a fence with pointed stakes around the camp, where they pitched their leather tents.

Horace padded round the camp. Amazing! It was huge. Groups of eight soldiers, that were from different regiments, slept in leather tents. The tent of the commanding officer was placed in the centre. Round the outside, there were latrines (toilets), cooking ovens and rubbish pits.

Horace listened. There were some exciting sounds that sent a shiver down his spine: the talking of the Roman soldiers, the clanging of their armour, the neighing of their horses and the clash of pots and pans. As night fell, a hush fell over the camp.

People in the army: legionnaires, auxiliary soldiers and some cavalry

Now Horace consulted his i-collar to find out more about the Roman army.

"The cavalry were soldiers who rode on horses. They were the eyes of the army, riding ahead of the legions and guarding them in battle."

"They were the highest paid Roman soldiers because they had to buy their own horses and equip them."

"The horse's saddle had two tall panels that gave the rider a secure seat but the harness was the same as we have today."

"The reigns were made of leather and linked to a bit that went into the horse's mouth."

"The riders had spurs attached to their shoes because stirrups hadn't been invented."

Next morning, Horace woke to cries of horror. The soldiers had received some news. The Celts were forming an army to support the Iceni tribe; they were in revolt and preparing to fight. In the misty morning, the Roman soldiers were getting ready to march. The commanding officer shouted out a command,

"Load the wagons, put in the tents and the camp kitchen. Prepare the giant catapults, (called ballistas), which fire the heavy bolts and stones at our enemy."

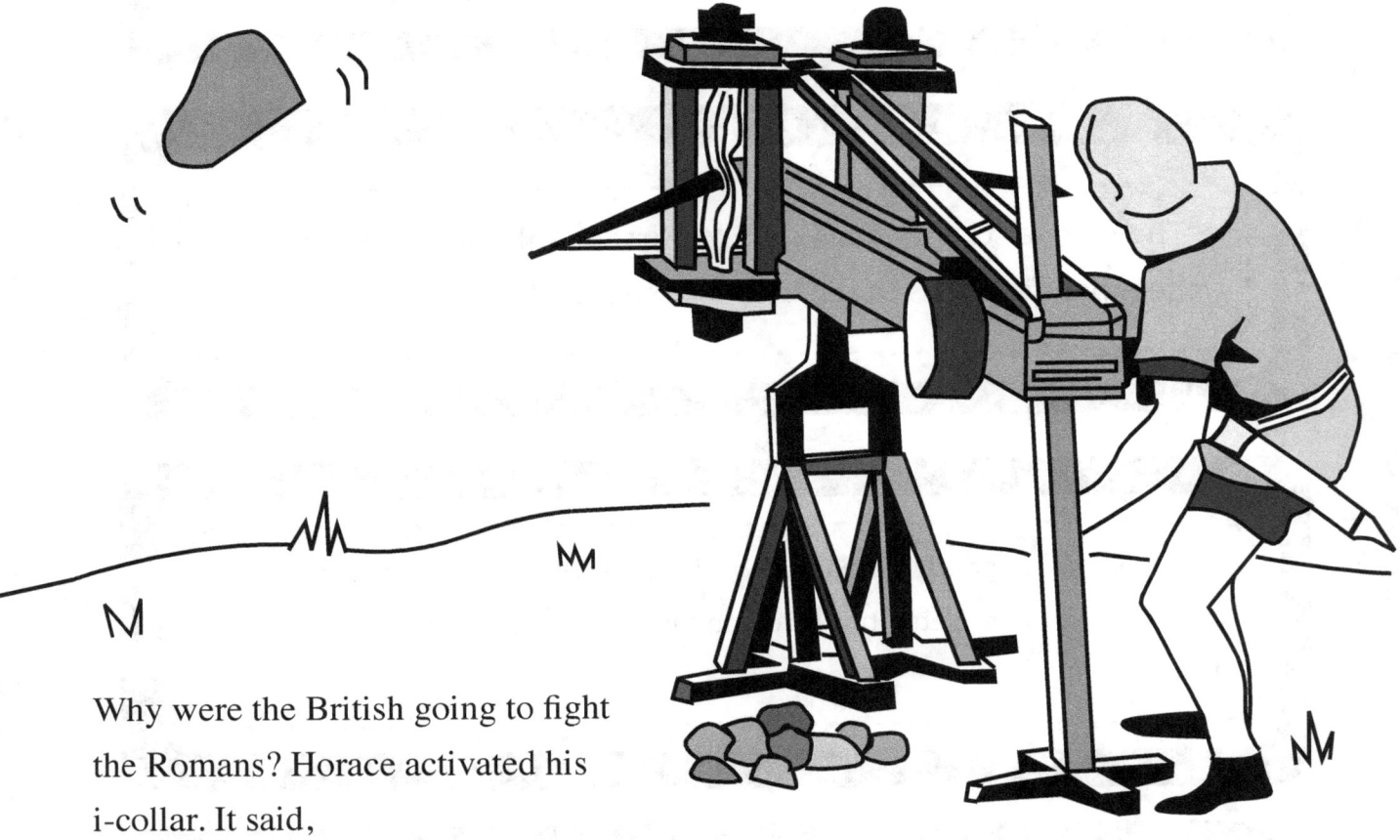

Why were the British going to fight the Romans? Horace activated his i-collar. It said,

> i-collar fact
> "Boudicca of the Iceni tribe was very angry that her husband, King Prasutagus, was dead. She was furious because he had helped the Romans, on the condition that they would look after his family, but now some soldiers from Colchester (Camulodunum) had whipped the queen and her daughters and stolen their land and treasure."

HORACE KNEW THIS MEANT <u>BIG TROUBLE</u>.

Horace accompanied them, riding in the soldier's pack. He felt proud to have joined them as an auxiliary (a foreigner serving in the Roman army) and he followed behind the Roman Governor, Suetonius Paulinus, who was up ahead with the cavalry. The long straight road echoed with the sound of the legions' marching feet.

Horace bounced up and down in the soldier's pack. Peering through the mist, he saw hills pass by, he saw fields pass by and he saw woods on each side. The soldiers marched on down Watling Street. Horace's head was spinning.

They stopped. One of the leaders shouted to a passer by,
"What news? Have you seen Boudicca?"
"No! but you won't miss her."
"What is she like?" whispered Horace to the soldier.
" She is tall, like a giant woman. Her eyes are fierce, fiendish and flash with fire. Her voice is hoarse, harsh and horrifying. She has a mane of bright red hair that hangs like rope around her hips and her torn, tatty tunic is covered by a thick cloak of wolf skin. She flies fearlessly along in her chariot, wielding an axe menacingly, screaming 'death to all Romans!'

"Terrifying!" thought Horace,
"absolutely terrifying!"

Watling Street: name for the Roman road between London and Wroxeter.

In an instant, Horace jumped down and padded to the front of the line to hear the latest news. That ferocious human, Boudicca, had already destroyed Londinium and Verulamium. In fact, her army had slaughtered seventy thousand people! Horace's ears twitched nervously. He couldn't believe what he was hearing.

The Roman army marched on.

There were ten thousand soldiers on the Roman side, compared to twenty thousand Celts on Boudicca's side.

A battle site was chosen. It was deep in the depths of the forest. What was that terrible noise? Were the Celts coming?

Horace hid under the bush; he was frightened of these terrifying Celtic tribes men with bright blue painted bodies and long, white stiff hair, who screamed out their battle cries ferociously.

Suddenly, the battle commenced; the soldiers were brave. Horace heard the war cries as the men charged, he heard the terrified neighs of the horses, he heard the crashing of the chariots as they smashed together and the banging of the swords and shields.

i-collar fact
"The British army was not as well protected as the Romans. They wore cloth tunics and cloaks, bronze helmets, shields and leather belts. Their scabbards were made of wood and they carried a sword and a spear."

Peeping out from behind the bush nervously, Horace witnessed Boudicca's army of foot soldiers charge the Romans. They were chopping - hacking - slaying. They were throwing stones from their slings. They were hurling spears to slaughter them. The British soldiers made every effort to break through the Roman lines - but they were not trained and disciplined like the Romans. Horace watched the clever Romans. They threw their lances and placed their shields flat like a tortoise's back, to stop those lethal British spears. Their cavalry thrashed the British soldiers until eight thousand men had fallen, but only four hundred Romans.

i-collar fact:

The British army had brought their whole families in wagons to watch the battle.

The battle raged for a long time. In the end, Boudicca was defeated. The brave woman was captured, but fearing she would be sold as a slave had swallowed poison and she was dead!

Now, the Romans were celebrating their victory so Horace stayed with his soldier friend and helped him eat his lunch of beans. He dozed lazily in the sun, tired after all that excitement. Crash! Bang! The Romans were building a fort determined to keep the Brits under control. It was nearly up... But, his eyes closed and before he knew it, he was back on the garden wall.

Easy Reader
Exercises

Week One

Monday: **Spelling Patterns**

Write the plural of the following words.

bean   head   spear   treasure   leader   ear

From the list below find a word that sounds the same.

bean   treasure   hear   reach   spear   leather

lean   clear   each   ear

- treasure   ....
- reach   ....
- ear   ....
- hear   ....
- bean   ....

From this list put the words into the correct boxes.

beans   reach   heavy   dead   realised   treasure

leather   hear   dear

NOUNS (things)	VERBS (doing words)	ADJECTIVES (describing words)

WEEK 1: Easy Reader

Tuesday: **Adverbs**

The majority of adverbs are found by *adding* '*ly*'

From the list find the correct adverbs for the sentences.

bravely   *easily*   *clearly*

greedily   *slowly*   *carefully*

happily   *quickly*   *mainly*

1. The soldiers shouted ....

2. Horace ate g....................

3. The soldiers marched q.................... to their camp.

4. Everyone h.................... ate their bread and beans.

5. They b.................... fought in the battle.

6. The clouds moved s.................... across the sky.

7. They could c.................... see the hills in the distance.

8. The soldiers c.................... packed their packs.

9. The workers were m.................... auxiliaries.

10. Horace e.................... jumped off the rocks.

WEEK 1: Easy Reader

Wednesday: **Direct Speech**

Put the speech into the following sentences.

Remember that capital letters are used to begin sentences and to begin direct speech. All speech and punctuation go inside the quotation (speech) marks.

1. The soldier fed Horace some beans. Perhaps the cat will bring us some good luck, he said.

2. What is that on your wrist? asked Horace.
   A purse, he replied.

3. Come on men, time to go, said the leader.

4. You carry my spade and I'll carry the cat, said the soldier.

5. The Roman Governor spoke to the soldiers. The British are in revolt, get ready to march in the morning.

6. Horace heard the soldier talking. King Prasutagus is dead and Queen Boudicca is very angry. She thought she could keep her lands.

7. How long will it take to get to Londinium? asked the soldiers.

8. It will take at least two weeks but many more men will join us on the way, said the Governor.

Imagine that you are a Roman Legionary (soldier). Copy the start of the letter into your book and finish it using information from the story or any other source.

Thursday

DEAR MOTHER,

I HAVE ARRIVED IN BRITAIN. THE WEATHER IS MISERABLE AND I AM LOOKING FORWARD TO REACHING OUR CAMP. I HAVE A SMART NEW UNIFORM AND NEW EQUIPMENT...

Friday: **British Warriors**

WEEK 1: Easy Reader

Label the parts of the soldiers uniform

Easy Reader
Exercises

Week Two

Monday: The Prepositions

The preposition is placed before a noun or a pronoun. It shows the relationship between nouns or pronouns in the same sentence.

Some common propositions

| to | of | in | from | with |
| upon | up | behind | below | |

Underline the propositions

e.g.   The boy must apologise to the lady.

1. The mother was proud of her son's success.
2. He placed the bat on the wall.
3. He put the book in the drawer.
4. His opinion differs from mine.
5. She takes great pride with her appearance.

Now copy out these sentences and use a preposition from the above list.

1. Horace lay in the sun .... the garden wall.
2. They piled the earth .... make a bank.
3. Horace listened .... the news.
4. Horace rode .... the soldier's pack.
5. The fence was made .... pointed stakes.

WEEK 2: Easy Reader

Tuesday: **Comprehension**

Re-read the story and answer the following questions in sentences.

1. Where did Horace find himself when he woke up?

   Horace found..

2. What did Horace see?

   Horace saw..

3. Who were the men?

   The men were..

4. What did they wear over their woollen tunics?

   Over their woollen tunics, they wore..

5. What did the soldiers have in their packs?

   Their packs contained...

6. Name any four more things they carried?

   They also carried...

7. What was the cloak also used for?

   His cloak was..

8. Why were the soldiers sent on ahead?

   The soldiers had been sent on ahead to......................................

9. How many men slept in the leather tents?

   There were..

10. Whose tent was in the middle of the camp?

    The...

WEEK 2: Easy Reader

Wednesday: Newspaper Report

In your best handwriting, copy out the report and fill in the gaps using words from the list below.

| heads | Celts | battle | fire |
| Claudius | town | cries | horses |

We are Victorious

We were in our houses when suddenly we heard the sound of h................ and chariots and the blood curdling c................ of the C............... In terror the citizens ran to the temple of C................, only to be killed by f...............

I watched from a nearby hill as the Celts thundered through the t............... burning it to the ground. We rallied our troops and chased after those madmen. We kept our h............... and fought a good b............... Slowly, we turned the tide and with so many dead around her Boudicca took poison and died. We were victorious

Put these lines in order using 1st letter, 2nd letter, 3rd letter, 4th letter and 5th letter.

Thursday: Alphabetical Order

1st letter
herald, arch, zebra, marble, jelly, rake

2nd letter
measles, music, march, monk, middle

3rd letter
drop, drudge, drill, drain, dress

4th letter
shrink, shrapnel, shrug, shred, shroud

5th letter
strict, string, stripe, stride, strike

Using your dictionary, look up the meanings of one word from each list and write them down.

WEEK 2: Easy Reader

Friday: **Boudicca's Revolt**

In AD 60 a British tribe called the Iceni revolted against Roman rule. The description of Queen Boudicca below was written by the Roman historian Dio.

> "SHE WAS HUGE WITH A HARSH VOICE. A GREAT MASS OF BRIGHT RED HAIR FELL TO HER KNEES. SHE WORE A GREAT TWISTED TORC AND A TUNIC OF MANY COLOURS, OVER WHICH WAS A THICK MANTLE FASTENED BY A BROOCH." DIO

Draw Queen Boudicca using the description above to help you. Underneath copy out Dio's description

Higher Level
Exercises

Week One

Monday: **Synonyms**

Underline the two words similar in meaning.

1. little, large, round, big
2. square, oval, round, circular
3. tall, heavy, small, weighty
4. short, up, down, wee
5. sleepy, surprise, astonish, attack
6. point, edge, direct, gone
7. river, fence, field, barrier
8. mix, take, blend, go
9. flat, hill, high, tall
10. attach, break, tie, shirt

Write out these sentences. In place of the underlined word, choose a word from the list below.

tried	*waste*	*round*	*started*
ghost	*smell*	*brave*	*least*
cheat	*short*		

1. The largest flowerbed is <u>circular</u> in shape.
2. The men <u>commenced</u> work at 9 a.m.
3. The terrified man saw an <u>apparition</u> coming towards him.
4. Arthur was praised for his <u>courageous</u> conduct.
5. Two boys <u>attempted</u> to lift the heavy bag.
6. We should not <u>squander</u> our money.
7. The <u>minimum</u> quantity supplied was one kilogram.
8. Do not <u>deceive</u> your friend.
9. It was a <u>brief</u> lecture.
10. There was a terrible <u>odour</u> coming from the kitchen.

WEEK 1: Higher Level

Tuesday: **Adverbs**

The majority of adverbs are found by *adding* '*ly*'

Put one of these adverbs in the following sentences.

loudly   *easily*   *clearly*   *bravely*   *greedily*

slowly   *carefully*   *happily*   *quickly*   *mainly*

1. The soldiers shouted ....
2. Horace ate ....
3. The soldiers marched .... to their camp.
4. Everyone .... ate their bread and beans.
5. They .... fought in the battle.
6. The clouds moved .... across the sky.
7. They could .... see the hills in the distance.
8. The soldiers .... packed their packs.
9. The workers were .... auxiliaries.
10. Horace .... jumped off the rocks.

Form adverbs from the following words. In some words you will need to change the 'y' to 'i' before adding 'ly'.

1. happy...
2. sweet...
3. true...
4. wide...
5. pure...
6. weary...
7. heavy...
8. ready

WEEK 1: Higher Level

Wednesday: **Direct Speech**

Capital letters are used to *begin sentences* and to *begin direct speech*. All speech and punctuation go inside the quotation (speech) marks.

Insert the necessary quotation marks in these sentences.

1. The soldier fed Horace some beans. Perhaps the cat will bring us some good luck, he said.

2. We need to find a larger field for the camp, said the soldier.

3. The soldier said, You carry the cat.

4. Don't forget your stakes, said the soldier.

5. They reached the site. Thank you said Horace.

6. What is the size of the camp? said Horace.
   It's twenty acres replied the man.

7. What is that on your wrist? asked Horace.
   A purse he replied.

8. The soldiers said the British are in revolt.

9. We are marching to Londinium said the Roman Governor.

10. One of the cavalry approached the leaders. What news? he asked.

WEEK 1: Higher Level

Thursday: **Double Consonants**

Choose the correct word for the following sentences from the list below.

| illustrate | carried | woollen | padded | approached |
| surrounded | warriors | collection | appeared | incorrect |

1. I............... the border in red and green.

2. I c............... my football boots in my bag.

3. The field was s............... by an electric fence.

4. Boudicca wore a w............... tunic.

5. Horace p............... round the camp.

6. I a............... the wild cat cautiously.

7. The Celtic w............... were painted blue.

8. My c............... of cards won a prize.

9. It a............... to him in a dream.

10. My answer was i...............

Now make up your own sentences with the following words. Remember that sentences must make sense.

| saddle | allow | collect | trapped | skidded |
| bitten | begged | robbed | expelled | planned |

WEEK 1: Higher Level

Friday: **British Warriors**

Label the parts of the soldiers uniform

Higher Level Exercises

Week Two

Monday: The Prepositions

The preposition is placed before a noun or a pronoun. It shows the relationship between nouns and pronouns in the same sentence.

Common propositions

about	above	across	after	against	along	among	without
around	at	before	behind	below	beneath	beside	witthin
between	beyond	by	down	during	except	for	with
from	in	near	of	off	on	over	upon
round	since	through	till	to	towards	under	up
underneath	until						

Copy and underline the prepositions in the following sentences.

e.g.   The boy must apologise **to** the lady.

1. The mother was proud of her son's success.
2. He placed the bat on the wall.
3. He put the book in the drawer.
4. His opinion differs from mine.
5. She takes great pride with her appearance.

Now write out these sentences and fill in the correct preposition from the list below.

on	from	up	to	of	by	to	on

1. Horace lay in the sun ... the garden wall.
2. They carried two pointed stakes ... ... make walls.
3. The land was free ... undergrowth.
4. They piled the earth ... make a bank.
5. The fence was made ... pointed stakes.
6. The steel strips were held together ... leather straps.
7. Horace listened ... the news.
8. Horace rode ... the soldier's pack.

Now make up your own sentences using – beneath, since and near.

WEEK 2: Higher Level

Tuesday: **Comprehension**

Read the facts about the Roman army on the next page and then answer the following questions.

1. Describe the pilum.
   ....

2. What did they make the walls of their camps with?
   ....

3. What was the marching camp also called?
   ....

4. What was the size of the camp?
   ....

5. Describe the soldiers' head armour.
   ....

6. Why were the soldier's purses hard to rob?
   ....

7. Why were the cavalry important?
   ....

8. How did the pommels on the horses harness help the cavalry soldiers?
   ....

9. What tribe did Boudicca belong to?
   ....

10. Describe some of the sounds Horace heard going round the camp?
    ....

A ROMAN ARMY ON THE MARCH

A Roman army, on the march, lived mainly on bread, beans and the odd bits of bacon and cheese. Each soldier carried a heavy pack on his shoulder which held: a tool kit to build camps, forts and roads, a bag of nails, an axe, a rope, a cooking pan, a cup and a leather bottle filled with water or wine. They also carried a turf cutter, a pickaxe and two pointed stakes to build the walls of their camp.

Their weapons were a javelin made of iron and wood, a double-edged blade dagger (a purgio), a short sword (a gladius) and a fearsome heavy javelin (a pilum). This had a narrow point that could pierce both shield and armour. The Roman soldier also carried a rectangular shield and a cloak, which doubled up as a blanket.

Some soldiers were sent along the road ahead of the rest of the legion, to find a dry piece of land free from undergrowth, to construct a 'marching camp' or entrenchment, as protection against surprise raids and wild animals.

When a suitable site for the entrenchment had been found, the soldiers dug a square ditch with rounded corners and piled the earth up to make a bank. This was covered with a fence (a palisade) of pointed stakes tied together. The entrance was protected by overlapping rampets, so the enemy would have to enter at an angle. Inside, the soldiers pitched their eight men leather tents in rows of ten.

The soldiers slept in leather tents; the commanding officers tent was in the middle. It was a mixed camp of legionnaires, auxillary soldiers in their armour and some cavalry. Horace was amazed at the size of the camp. This one was twenty acres, which is as big as fifteen football pitches.

The soldiers were in full army kit. Over their rough woollen tunics, they wore body armour made of thin strips of steel fitted with hooks and hinges down the front. These strips were held together by leather straps and on the inside of the armour they also had metal shoulder pads.

The soldiers' heads were protected by metal helmets, with hinged cheek pieces and a metal rim sticking out at the back. The armour was very heavy.

On their feet, the soldiers wore strong leather strip sandals, with patterns of iron hobnails underneath to take the weight and the miles of marching. On their wrists they carried cash in a leather or bronze purse. Worn like a bracelet, it could only be opened when it was taken off, so it was hard to rob.

The cavalry soldiers were the eyes of the army, scouting ahead of the legions, guarding their flanks in battle and pursuing and harassing defeated enemies. They were also the highest paid Roman soldiers, partly because they had to pay for and equip their own horses.

The harness was much the same as today. Leather reigns and a bridle were linked to a bit which went in the horse's mouth. The riders used spurs attached to their shoes. The stirrup had not yet been invented. Instead the saddles had tall pommels, which gave riders a secure seat.

As Horace padded around, he found the different sounds of the camp exciting - the clash of armour, the neighing of horses and the clanging of pots and pans. The soldiers were talking about their day. Horace listed to the news. The British were in revolt. The Catuvellauni, the Trinovantes and others were all going to join the Iceni tribe, led by Boudicca. The smell of food made Horace's whiskers twitch. He thought, "The Roman army seems very organised."

WEEK 2: Higher Level

Wednesday

Imagine that you are a Roman Legionary (soldier). Copy the start of the letter into your book and finish it using information from the story or any other sources.

> DEAR MOTHER,
>
> I HAVE ARRIVED IN BRITAIN. THE WEATHER IS MISERABLE AND I AM LOOKING FORWARD TO REACHING OUR CAMP. I HAVE A SMART NEW UNIFORM AND NEW EQUIPMENT...

Battle with Boudicca

Thursday: Poetry Writing

You are going to write a poem about the battle between the Romans and the Celtic Queen Boudicca.

First find as many powerful verbs as you can to use in your poem. Here are some examples.

screaming	charging
fighting	hacking
pounding	....
....	....
....	....
....	....

Can you think of any more?

Now put the adjectives and nouns together.

e.g. *charging chariots*
furious warrior
Celtic charge
fierce battle
bloodcurdling screams
pounding swords

Build up some phrases:

e.g. *charging chariots thunder towards each other*

Now use the ideas to help you write your poem.

WEEK 2: Higher Level

Friday

Imagine that you are a reporter for either a Roman or Celtic newspaper. Your task is to write a report about Boudicca's uprising. Your report could start something like this...

QUEEN BOUDICCA HAS DISAPPOINTED!

Following the tragic defeat and capture of Queen Boudicca yesterday, rumours are circulating that she has taken a lethal dose of poison. The events leading up to her death are a terrible reminder of the strength and ruthlessness of the Roman occupation...

Would this report be from a Roman or Celtic point of view? Why? How could you change it to show that you are writing from the other point of view?

You need to include the answers to the following questions in your report. You must write at least four sentences to answer each question.

1. Why did Boudicca fight against the Romans?

2. What happened at Colchester?

3. Which towns did Boudicca's army then attack?

4. Why did the Roman army not stop these attacks?

5. Where did the two armies finally meet?

6. Describe the battle. Use plenty of detail.

Remind yourself of the main points of the story to help you to write your newspaper report.

In AD61, the Romans were occupying Britain...

- The King of the Iceni tribe died.

- He had made a plan, that when he died, his wife would rule and the Romans would help her, but the Roman tax collectors came from Colchester and stole all her lands and treasures.

- Boudicca called for an army and many Celts came because the Romans had also taken their lands and made them pay taxes.

- Boudicca marched to attack Roman Colchester. They killed many people and burnt Colchester down.

- Boudicca and her army then marched to London and set it on fire. Seventy thousand people died. Many ran away because they were frightened.

- Next, Boudicca marched to Verulamium (St Albans).

- The Romans had a problem. The nearest legions were miles away. The ninth legion marched from Lindum (Lincoln), but were attacked and destroyed by the Celts.

- The Roman Governor Seutonius was in Anglesey fighting the Druids. When he heard the news he marched towards London.

- Boudicca led her army out of London towards the Roman army. The Britons were so sure they would win, that they brought their families to watch the battle. They drove their carts into a great half circle round the battlefield, with the women and children standing in them to get a good view.

- Boudicca rode round her army in a chariot. "We British are used to women commanders in war," she said. "I am not fighting for my kingdom. I am fighting to be free."

- We do not know where the final battle took place. It was probably somewhere along Watling Street (the road from London to Wroxeter). The Romans had ten thousand men. Boudicca had many times that number. In fact, there were ten Britons to every Roman, but the Romans were well trained and well armed. They each had two javelins, a shield and a sword.

- The trumpets sounded and thousands of Britons rushed at the Roman army. When they were fifty metres away, the Romans moved at once like a machine. Six thousand javelins flew through the air and then six thousand more. The first line of Britons fell. Then the Romans pulled out their swords and charged.

- After many hours the Romans won.

- In the final battle eighty thousand Britons were killed. The Romans only lost four hundred men.

- Some Britons escaped but the Romans killed every Briton they caught - even the families who were watching.

- Boudicca killed herself by taking poison.

- The Romans were back in charge.

Prefixes and Suffixes

These prefixes mean

a	on	afloat, ashore
ante	before	anteroom
bi/bis	two/twice	bicycle, biped, bisect
circum	around	circumference, circuit
de	down	descend, describe
dif/dis	apart/not	different, disagree, disappear
ex	out of	export, extract
fore	before	forecast, foretell
im/in	in/into	import, include
inter	between	interval
mis	wrong	mistake, misjudge
ob	against	object, obstruct
post	after	postpone, post war, postscript
pre	before	predict, prepare
re	back	retake, return, retrace
sub	under	subway, submarine
trans	across	transfer, transport
un	no, without	unfit, unknown, unpaid
vice	instead	vice captain

Identify the prefixes in the words in the following sentences

1. The boat was **a**float.
2. She had a red **b**icycle.
3. The tree had the largest circumference.
4. They were asked to describe the picture.
5. They did not disagree with the result.
6. They decided to export more wheat.
7. The forecast was for rain.
8. We had to include an apple in our lunch.
9. The interval was fifteen minutes.
10. It was a mistake she said.
11. The bricks made an obstruction to the path.
12. We had to postpone the match.
13. We had to prepare for our exams.
14. We bought a return ticket.
15. The subway was underneath the railway line.
16. The footballer had a transfer to another club.
17. The meat was unfit to eat.
18. She was excited at being vice captain.

Prefixes and Suffixes

These suffixes mean

ly	to make	nervously
able	capable of being	moveable, eatable, incredible
ant	one who	assistant, servant
el/et/ette	little	satchel, locket
er/eer/ier	one who	banker, engineer, furrier
ess	the female	goddess, princess, waitress, lioness
fy	to make	glorify, purify, simplify
less	without	careless, guiltless, merciless
ling	little	gosling, seedling, darling
ment	state of being	merriment, enjoyment
oon/on	large	balloon
ory	a place for	factory, laboratory
ous	full of	famous, glorious, momentous

Identify the suffixes in the words in the following sentences

1. The meal was uneat**able**.
2. The servant cleaned the room.
3. The waitress dropped the tray.
4. Their careless attitude lost them the match.
5. There was great merriment at the party.
6. The experiment was to purify the water.
7. The factory gates were closed.
8. It was a glorious sunset.
9. The gosling followed its mother to the pond.
10. The hot air balloon floated gracefully across the sky.

Double Consonants

hammer   dagger   tabby   purred   battle

bottle   saddle   apple   pattern   wall

called   yellow   rippled   terrible   cabbage

paddle   dropped   kitten   filled   collect

padded

Choose the correct double consonant word for the following sentences. Remember that sentences must make sense.

1. Knock the nail in with the ....
2. The soldier carried a ....
3. The cat ....
4. I have a .... cat.
5. .... your books please.
6. What a good .... you have made.
7. The sun is ....
8. I like to .... in the sea.
9. I .... my .... with water.
10. Eat your .... said mum.
11. The .... played with the wool.
12. I had an .... in my lunch box.
13. The Romans and Celts fought a ....
14. I .... my dog back.
15. We had a .... storm last night.
16. I .... my drink.
17. .... the horse please.
18. The waves .... across the pond.
19. I sat on the ....
20. The lion .... across his cage.

ANSWERS

EASY READER EXERCISES

MONDAY: Week One

| beans | heads | spears | treasures | leaders | ears |

treasure	leather
reach	each
ear	clear
hear	spear
bean	lean

NOUNS (things)	VERBS (doing words)	ADJECTIVES (describing words)
beans	reach	heavy
treasure	realised	dead
leather	hear	clear

TUESDAY: Week One

1. The soldiers shouted loudly.
2. Horace ate greedily.
3. The soldiers marched quickly to their camp.
4. Everyone happily ate their bread and beans.
5. They bravely fought in the battle.
6. The clouds moved slowly across the sky.
7. They could clearly see the hills in the distance.
8. The soldiers carefully packed their packs.
9. The workers were mainly auxiliaries.
10. Horace easily jumped off the rocks.

WEDNESDAY: Week One

1. The soldier fed Horace some beans. "Perhaps the cat will bring us good luck," he said.
2. "What is that on your wrist?" asked Horace.
   "A purse," he replied.
3. "Come on men, time to go," said the leader.
4. "You carry my spade and I'll carry the cat," said the soldier.
5. The Roman Governor spoke to the soldiers. "The British are in revolt, get ready to march in the morning."
6. Horace heard the soldier talking. "King Prasutagus is dead and Queen Boudicca is very angry, she thought she could keep her land."
7. "How long will it take to get to Londinium?" asked the soldier.
8. "It will take at least two weeks, but more men will join us on the way," said the Governor.

ANSWERS

EASY READER EXERCISES

FRIDAY: Week One

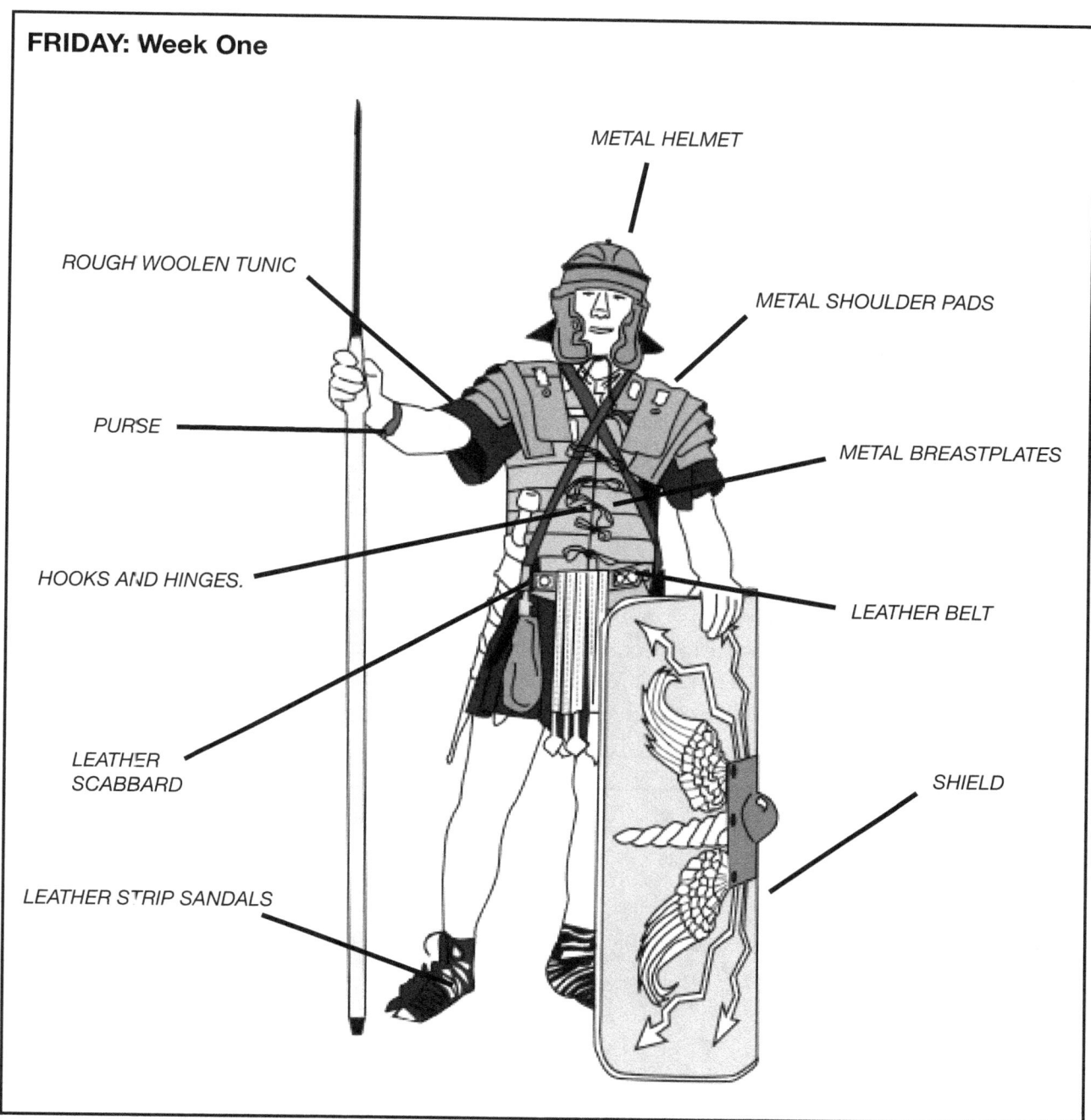

- METAL HELMET
- ROUGH WOOLEN TUNIC
- METAL SHOULDER PADS
- PURSE
- METAL BREASTPLATES
- HOOKS AND HINGES.
- LEATHER BELT
- LEATHER SCABBARD
- SHIELD
- LEATHER STRIP SANDALS

Monday: Week Two

1. The mother was proud <u>of</u> her son's success.
2. He placed the bat <u>on</u> the wall.
3. He put the book <u>in</u> the drawer.
4. His opinion differs <u>from</u> mine.
5. She takes great pride <u>with</u> her appearance.

....

1. Horace lay in the sun on the garden wall.
2. They piled the earth up to make a bank.
3. Horace listened to the news.
4. Horace rode on the soldiers pack.
5. The fence was made of pointed stakes.

ANSWERS

EASY READER EXERCISES

TUESDAY: Week Two

1. Horace found himself curled up by a large, flat rock.
2. Horace saw some men dropping their shields by the side of the road.
3. The men were Roman foot soldiers.
4. Over their woollen tunics, they wore body armour made of thin strips of steel filled with hooks and hinges, with metal shoulder pads and breastplates.
5. The soldier's packs contained a tool kit, a bag of nails, bread, cheese, beans, bacon and water.
6. The soldiers also carried an axe, a rope, a cooking pan, a cup, a turf cutter, a pickaxe, a javelin, a short sword called a gladius, a shield and a cloak.
7. His cloak was also used as a blanket.
8. The soldiers had been sent on ahead to find some dry, clear land to build a marching camp.
9. There were eight men to a tent.
10. The commanding officer's tent was in the middle of the camp.

WEDNESDAY: Week Two

We were in our houses when suddenly we heard the sound of **horses** and chariots and the blood curdling **cries** of the **Celts**. In terror the citizens ran to the Temple of **Claudius**, only to be killed by **fire**. I watched from a nearby hill as the Celts thundered through the **town** burning it to the ground. We rallied our troops and chased after those madmen. We kept our **heads** and fought a good **battle**. Slowly we turned the tide and with so many dead around her Boudicca took poison and died. We were victorious.

THURSDAY: Week Two

1st Letter

arch   herald   jelly   marble   rake   zebra

2nd Letter

march   measles   middle   monk   music

3rd Letter

drain   dress   drill   drop   drudge

4th Letter

shrapnel   shred   shrink   shroud   shrug

5th Letter

strict   stride   strike   string   stripe

ANSWERS

HIGHER LEVEL EXERCISES

MONDAY: Week One

large	big
round	circular
heavy	weighty
short	wee
surprise	astonish
pointed	direct
fence	barrier
mix	blend
high	tall
attach	tie

1. The largest flowerbed is **round** in shape.
2. The men **started** work at 9am.
3. The terrified man saw a **ghost** coming towards him.
4. Arthur was praised for his **brave** conduct.
5. Two boys **tried** to lift the heavy bag.
6. We should not **waste** our money.
7. The **least** quantity supplied is one kilogram.
8. Do not **cheat** your friend.
9. It was a **short** lecture.
10. There was a terrible **smell** coming from the kitchen.

TUESDAY: Week One

1. The soldiers shouted loudly.
2. Horace ate greedily.
3. The soldiers marched quickly to their camp.
4. Everyone happily ate their bread and beans.
5. They bravely fought in the battle.
6. The clouds moved slowly across the sky.
7. They could clearly see the hills in the distance.
8. The soldiers carefully packed their packs.
9. The workers were mainly auxiliaries.
10. Horace easily jumped off the rocks.

happily	sweetly	truely	widely
purely	wearily	heavily	readily

ANSWERS

HIGHER LEVEL EXERCISES

WEDNESDAY: Week One

1. The soldier fed Horace some beans, "Perhaps the cat will bring us good luck," he said.
2. "We need to find a larger field for the camp," said the soldier.
3. The soldier said, "You carry the cat."
4. "Don't forget your stakes," said the soldier.
5. They reached the site, "Thank you," said Horace.
6. "What is the size of the camp?" said Horace.
   "It's twenty acres," replied the man.
7. "What is that on your wrist?" asked Horace.
   "A purse," he replied.
8. The soldiers said, "The British are in revolt."
9. "We are marching to Londinium," said the Roman Governor.
10. One of the cavalry approached the leaders. "What news," he asked.

THURSDAY: Week One

1. Illustrate the border in red and green.
2. I carried my football boots in my bag.
3. The field was surrounded by an electric fence.
4. Boudicca wore a woollen tunic.
5. Horace padded round the camp.
6. I approached the wild cat cautiously.
7. The Celtic warriors were painted blue.
8. My collection of cards won a prize.
9. It appeared to him in a dream.
10. My answer was incorrect.

FRIDAY: Week One

See the answers to easy reader exercises (Friday: Week One).

MONDAY: Week Two

1. The mother was proud **of** her son's success.
2. He placed the bat **on** the wall.
3. He put the book **in** the drawer.
4. His opinion differs **from** mine.
5. She takes great pride **with** her appearance.

....

1. Horace lay in the sun on the garden wall.
2. They carried two pointed stakes to make walls.
3. The land was free from undergrowth.
4. They piled the earth up to make a bank.
5. The fence was made of pointed stakes.
6. The steel strips were held together by leather straps.
7. Horace listened to the news.
8. Horace rode on the soldier's packs.

ANSWERS

HIGHER LEVEL EXERCISES

TUESDAY: Week Two

1. The pilum is a heavy javelin with a narrow point that can pierce shields and armour.
2. The soldiers carried two pointed stakes each to make the walls.
3. Marching camps were also called entrenchments.
4. The camp was twenty acres, which is about the same as fifteen football pitches.
5. The soldiers' heads were protected by metal helmets. They had hinged cheek pieces and a metal rim sticking out at the back.
6. They wore a leather or bronze purse on their wrist like a bracelet. It could only be opened when it was taken off.
7. The cavalry were the eyes of the army, scouting ahead of the legions and guarding their flanks in battle, pursuing and harassing defeated enemies.
8. The stirrup had not yet been invented. Instead the saddle had tall pommels that gave the rider a secure seat.
9. Boudicca belonged to the Iceni tribe.
10. Horace heard the clash of armour, the neighing of horses and the clanging of pots and pans.

ANSWERS

EXTRA WORK

Prefixes

1. The boat was **a**float.
2. She had a red **bi**cycle.
3. The tree had the largest **circum**ference.
4. They were asked to **de**scribe the picture.
5. They did not **dis**agree with the result.
6. They decided to **ex**port more wheat.
7. The **fore**cast was for rain.
8. We had to **in**clude an apple in our lunch.
9. The **inter**val was fifteen minutes.
10. It was a **mis**take she said.
11. The bricks made an **ob**struction to the path.
12. We had to **post**pone the match.
13. We had to **pre**pare for our exams.
14. We bought a **re**turn ticket.
15. The **sub**way was underneath the railway line.
16. The footballer had a **trans**fer to another club.
17. The meat was **un**fit to eat.
18. She was excited at being **vice** captain.

Suffixes

1. The meal was uneat**able**.
2. The serv**ant** cleaned the room.
3. The waitr**ess** dropped the tray.
4. Their care**less** attitude lost them the match.
5. There was great merri**ment** at the party.
6. The experiment was to puri**fy** the water.
7. The fact**ory** gates were closed.
8. It was a glor**ious** sunset.
9. The gos**ling** followed its mother to the pond.
10. The hot air ball**oon** floated gracefully across the sky.

Double Consonants

1. Knock the nail in with the hammer.
2. The soldier carried a dagger.
3. The cat purred.
4. I have a tabby cat.
5. Collect your books please.
6. What a good pattern you have made.
7. The sun is yellow.
8. I like to paddle in the sea.
9. I filled my bottle with water.
10. Eat your cabbage said mum.
11. The kitten played with the wool.
12. I had an apple in my lunch box.
13. The Romans and Celts fought a battle.
14. I called my dog back.
15. We had a terrible storm last night.
16. I dropped my drink.
17. Saddle the horse please.
18. The waves rippled across the pond.
19. I sat on the wall.
20. The lion padded across his cage.

www.ingramcontent.com/pod-product-compliance
Lightning Source LLC
Chambersburg PA
CBHW050716090526
44587CB00019B/3401